REPORTS THAT STUDENTS LOVE TO WRITE AND TEACHERS LOVE TO READ

Content- and Skills-Based Reinforcement,
Enrichment, and Assessment

by Imogene Forte and Sandra Schurr

Incentive Publications, Inc.
Nashville, Tennessee

Illustrated by Marta J. Drayton
Cover by Marta Drayton and Joe Shibley
Edited by Jan Keeling

ISBN 0-86530-404-1

Table of Contents

Preface

Writing a report may not seem like a lot of fun. But knowing how to write a good report is an essential part of learning. It offers a way to organize and summarize research findings, to continue to learn while you summarize, and to communicate what you have learned to others. Is there any way to make report-writing fun?

There are lots of ways! You can have students create an Anti–Coloring Book Report, where research findings are related to a drawing that includes just enough detail to stimulate the imagination to do more. An Artifact Show-and-Tell Report connects oral communication and exploration with physical objects that have interest and meaning. Students can create a series of letters or postcards for a Letter or Postcard Report, putting a personal touch on research. A Notebook Field Report allows the student to collect many different types of information and record them in many different ways while enjoying real-life experiences. And how could a Comic Strip Report not be fun?

Innovative report formats can reinforce learning while maintaining a high level of interest in both the creator of the report and the reader of the report. When visual or oral presentation is a part of a report, a little planning can lead to a dynamic, informative presentation.

Each report format section begins with an information/instruction page for the teacher. This page defines the report format, tells its purpose, and gives an overview of how the report is created.

One or two student pages for each format are usually planning outlines or forms that are invaluable for planning and creating the report. A student page can be recognized by the copyright line at the bottom of the page.

Finally, each report format has an Assessment Rubric, a self-evaluating page with imaginative rating scales that the student can use to rate the quality of the different report elements. It is at this point that the student reflects on the relevance, organization, grammar, interest, and creativity used and displayed in his or her report. At the bottom of the page are spaces for comments by the student and by the teacher.

There need be no sacrifice of content, research skills, or creative thinking and writing skills when a student is asked to prepare an enjoyable report. Students love to make these reports—and you will love to read them!

The ABC Report

One way to organize information for a report is to use the alphabet as a springboard for writing a set of facts related to the topic. An ABC report contains 26 short statements or paragraphs about facts that have a common theme. The report should be given a title that gives the reader a clue to what the report is about. Then follows a series of substantive sentences arranged in alphabetical order.

After determining a subject for the report, the student should begin researching, collecting, and recording relevant information on notecards, one fact per notecard. The facts should be written or rephrased so that a key word in the fact begins with one of the letters of the alphabet. When arranging words alphabetically this way, there may be a few letters that are "difficult" to use (such as X, Y, Z). If the student can't think of a word that begins with a "difficult" letter, the letter can be used by phrasing a sentence creatively. For example:

Q is for Quick ideas about . . .

X is for eXamples of . . .

U is for Understanding . . .

W is for Ways to . . .

Z is for the Zest (the main character) showed when . . .

Key Words for the **ABC Report**

Name: _____

Topic: _____

A _____
_____
_____
_____
_____

B _____
_____
_____
_____
_____

C _____
_____
_____
_____
_____

D _____
_____
_____
_____
_____

E _____
_____
_____
_____
_____

F _____
_____
_____
_____
_____

G _____
_____
_____
_____
_____

H _____
_____
_____
_____
_____

I _____
_____
_____
_____
_____

J _____
_____
_____
_____
_____

K _____
_____
_____
_____
_____

L _____
_____
_____
_____
_____

M _____
_____
_____
_____
_____

Reports Students Love to Write
©1999 by Incentive Publications, Inc., Nashville, TN.

Name: _____

Topic: _____

N _____
_____
_____
_____
_____

O _____
_____
_____
_____
_____

P _____
_____
_____
_____
_____

Q _____
_____
_____
_____
_____

R _____
_____
_____
_____
_____

S _____
_____
_____
_____
_____

T _____
_____
_____
_____
_____

U _____
_____
_____
_____
_____

V _____
_____
_____
_____
_____

W _____
_____
_____
_____
_____

X _____
_____
_____
_____
_____

Y _____
_____
_____
_____
_____

Z _____
_____
_____
_____
_____

Reports Students Love to Write

The ABC Report

1. Quality of Report Format
I wrote an important and relevant fact or idea for each letter of the alphabet.

YES	NO
SOMEWHAT	

2. Quality of Information
My 26 informational items seem to flow in a logical sequence.

YES	NO
SOMEWHAT	

3. Grammar
The report is written with no grammar or spelling errors.

YES	NO
SOMEWHAT	

4. Interest
The report is interesting to read.

YES	NO
SOMEWHAT	

5. Graphics/Creativity
I included sufficient graphics to make my report colorful.

YES	NO
SOMEWHAT	

Comments by Student: _____

_____

_____

_____

Comments by Teacher: _____

_____

_____

_____

Reports Students Love to Write   ©1999 by Incentive Publications, Inc., Nashville, TN.

Anti–Coloring Book Report

The coloring book format makes an interesting report. Such a report has a number of paired pages that present information about the topic on one side and a large outline drawing to color on the opposite side of the sheet. It is important that the drawing outline be related to the corresponding information page. Sometimes the drawings can be almost completed, requiring the reader only to add minor details and select colors. At other times a drawing can be a starter idea that requires the reader to complete the outline before coloring it in. This last method is the "anti–coloring book" concept. It challenges the reader to do more than provide simple enhancements for someone else's work.

The student should select a topic or theme and research it, making careful notes of the important ideas. These ideas should then be rewritten as a series of paragraphs which can be put together according to a particular scope and sequence, offering the reader a comprehensive overview of the subject. Each idea is written on one side of an 8½" x 11" piece of drawing paper with a corresponding picture sketched on the other side. These pages can be stapled or bound together into a coloring book (or anti–coloring book). Each book should be given front and back covers and a title page as well.

Planning Guide for **Anti–Coloring Book Report**

Name: _____

Topic: _____

Page One

1. Subtopic to write about: _____

   _____

2. Related drawing idea: _____

   _____

Page Two

1. Subtopic to write about: _____

   _____

2. Related drawing idea: _____

   _____

Page Three

1. Subtopic to write about: _____

   _____

2. Related drawing idea: _____

   _____

Page Four

1. Subtopic to write about: _____

   _____

2. Related drawing idea: _____

   _____

Page Five

1. Subtopic to write about: _____

   _____

2. Related drawing idea: _____

   _____

Reports Students Love to Write   ©1999 by Incentive Publications, Inc., Nashville, TN.

Planning Guide for **Anti–Coloring Book Report**

Name: _____

Topic: _____

Page Six

1. Subtopic to write about: _____

   _____

2. Related drawing idea: _____

   _____

Page Seven

1. Subtopic to write about: _____

   _____

2. Related drawing idea: _____

   _____

Page Eight

1. Subtopic to write about: _____

   _____

2. Related drawing idea: _____

   _____

Page Nine

1. Subtopic to write about: _____

   _____

2. Related drawing idea: _____

   _____

Page Ten

1. Subtopic to write about: _____

   _____

2. Related drawing idea:. _____

   _____

Reports Students Love to Write

Assessment Rubric

---

1. Quality of Report Format
Covers, title page, paired pages with paragraphs of information on topic and outline drawings are all present.

Out of the Gate   Home Stretch

Second Lap

---

2. Quality of Information
My report presents information in a logical sequence of paragraphs, giving a comprehensive overview of the subject.

Out of the Gate   Home Stretch

Second Lap

---

3. Grammar
My report is written with no grammar or spelling errors.

Out of the Gate   Home Stretch

Second Lap

---

4. Interest
My report is interesting to read and color.

Out of the Gate   Home Stretch

Second Lap

---

5. Graphics/Creativity
The arrangement of my report and the outline drawings are well done and effective.

Out of the Gate   Home Stretch

Second Lap

Comments by Student: _____

_____

_____

_____

Comments by Teacher: _____

_____

_____

_____

Artifact Show-and-Tell Report

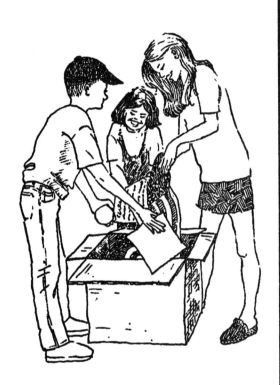

The Artifact Show-and-Tell Report provides an excellent base for cooperative learning, partnership, or individual independent study projects. This report is built around a bag or box full of related artifacts as the basis for the presentation of information. The artifacts can be small objects, pencil drawings, photographs, letters, diagrams, charts, recipes, souvenirs, samples, or other articles that have some significant relationship to the person, place, or thing under study. Each artifact is used as a springboard for introducing and explaining something about the report topic.

After a topic has been chosen for the report, the student or student group collects, photographs, draws, or constructs a set of artifacts that are directly related to the subject. Each artifact should be numbered in order of the planned presentation. Each should be accompanied by a large tag or file card explaining the significance of that artifact to the overall subject.

A plain grocery bag, shopping bag, or cardboard box can be decorated with the title and theme of the report. It becomes the package for housing the artifacts during the oral presentation of the information.

Planning Guide for **Artifact Show-and-Tell Report**

Name: _____

Topic: _____

Artifact One: _____
1. What is it and/or why is it important? _____
   _____
2. How is it used and/or who values it? _____
   _____

Artifact Two: _____
1. What is it and/or why is it important? _____
   _____
2. How is it used and/or who values it? _____
   _____

Artifact Three: _____
1. What is it and/or why is it important? _____
   _____
2. How is it used and/or who values it? _____
   _____

Artifact Four: _____
1. What is it and/or why is it important? _____
   _____
2. How is it used and/or who values it? _____
   _____

Artifact Five: _____
1. What is it and/or why is it important? _____
   _____
2. How is it used and/or who values it? _____
   _____

Planning Guide for **Artifact Show-and-Tell Report**

Name: _____

Topic: _____

Artifact Six: _____

1. What is it and/or why is it important? _____

   _____

2. How is it used and/or who values it? _____

   _____

Artifact Seven: _____

1. What is it and/or why is it important? _____

   _____

2. How is it used and/or who values it? _____

   _____

Artifact Eight: _____

1. What is it and/or why is it important? _____

   _____

2. How is it used and/or who values it? _____

   _____

Artifact Nine: _____

1. What is it and/or why is it important? _____

   _____

2. How is it used and/or who values it?

   _____

Artifact Ten: _____

1. What is it and/or why is it important? _____

   _____

2. How is it used and/or who values it? _____

   _____

Reports Students Love to Write

Assessment Rubric

Rating Scale

✔+   ✔   ✔-

---

1. Quality of Report Format

Oral presentation uses artifacts related to the topic, with tags or file cards for each artifact explaining its significance, and a decorated bag.   **Rating:** _____

---

2. Quality of Information

Oral presentation is well researched and artifacts are very relevant to information on the topic.   **Rating:** _____

---

3. Grammar

Grammar of presentation and grammar and spelling of tags or file cards is correct.   **Rating:** _____

---

4. Interest

Artifacts and oral presentation are smoothly presented, interesting, clear, and informative.   **Rating:** _____

---

5. Graphics/Creativity

Artifacts are creatively chosen and ordered to convey topic information.   **Rating:** _____

Comments by Student: _____

_____

_____

_____

Comments by Teacher: _____

_____

_____

_____

     ©1999 by Incentive Publications, Inc., Nashville, TN.

The Bookmark Report

In recent years, bookmarks have become interesting sources of information, advertising, and personal messages. These bookmarks, sold in many retail and catalog outlets, vary significantly in size and design. They make popular gifts, reminders, teaching tools, or springboards for poems and wise sayings. In the classroom, student- and teacher-designed bookmarks have proven to be a cost-effective and motivational teaching tool.

The Bookmark Report should consist of a set of eight to ten bookmarks created by the student, all related to a given theme or topic. Each bookmark covers a different element or segment of the selected topic, stating key facts or ideas to be reported. The bookmarks should be oversized to allow for maximum content coverage. Bookmarks can be made from posterboard, file folders, 5 x 8 file cards, or cardstock. Information and/or directions should be printed or typed and should be enhanced with some type of minimal art work.

The Bookmark Report

Name: _____

Topic: _____

Assessment Rubric

Rating Scale

1	2	3	4	5
Throwing Tomatoes		Round of Applause		Standing Ovation

1. Quality of Report Format

The topic of my set of bookmarks is important and
the bookmarks convey topic information well.

Rating: _____

2. Quality of Information

My bookmarks were well researched and convey key information.

Rating: _____

3. Grammar

The grammar and spelling of my bookmarks is correct.

Rating: _____

4. Interest

My bookmarks are attractive and entertaining enough to make them of high interest.

Rating: _____

5. Graphics/Creativity

The art work on my bookmarks is of good quality.

Rating: _____

Comments by Student: _____

_____

_____

_____

Comments by Teacher: _____

_____

_____

_____

Reports Students Love to Write

The Calendar Report

People around the world have come to see a calendar as both a practical reference tool and an art form. Calendars are popular as gift items and may be purchased in a wide range of styles from cartoon and pop art to fine art. They depict a variety of topics ranging from hobbies and sports to birds and historical monuments.

A Calendar Report can be created in one of two ways. It can be a detailed calendar of facts for each day of a designated month, or it can be a detailed calendar of facts for each month of the year. Either way, the calendar should have a special focus and should include both information and graphics.

Once the student has selected a research topic, the calendar format should be selected. The report can range in size from a wall-type calendar that has twelve double pages, one for each month of the year, to a desk-size format that has 28 to 31 single pages, one for each day of the selected month. The calendar can be created using plain drawing paper, shelf paper, or copy paper, and it can be given a durable cover made from a file folder or posterboard. A wall-type calendar should have several paragraphs of related copy on the top half of the calendar, along with a graphic or illustration; the bottom half of the calendar should show the appropriate calendar format for each month. The desk-size calendar should have a key fact or idea printed on each page; the day of the month should be printed in a large numerical form alongside a smaller graphic or drawing.

The top half of the wall-type calendar includes:
- several paragraphs of related information
- related graphics, pictures, or illustrations

The bottom half of the wall-type calendar includes:
- the calendar format for each month
- the month and days filled in appropriately (master calendar on page 26)

The calendar may be be attached at the top to flip or in the middle to fold over.

The desk-type calendar includes:
- key fact or idea printed on each page
- the month
- the day of the month printed in large numerical form
- small graphic or drawing

The desk-type calendar may be attached at the top with staples or with string threaded through punched holes.

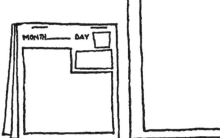

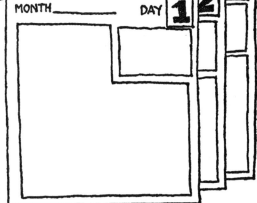

Reports Students Love to Write

Planning Form for the **Wall-Type Calendar Report**

	SUNDAY	MONDAY	TUESDAY	WEDNESDAY	THURSDAY	FRIDAY	SATURDAY

Reports Students Love to Write   ©1999 by Incentive Publications, Inc., Nashville, TN.

Month _____ Day

Month _____ Day

Month _____ Day

Month _____ Day

Assessment Rubric

	Not Yet	Trying	OK	Almost There	Wow!
1. Quality of Report Format My report is a calendar, wall type or desk size, with cover and graphics/illustrations.	1	2	3	4	5
2. Quality of Information The facts and ideas in my calendar show significant research on my topic.	1	2	3	4	5
3. Grammar There are no spelling or grammar errors in my calendar.	1	2	3	4	5
4. Interest The sequence and presentation of my topic are logical and engaging.	1	2	3	4	5
5. Graphics/Creativity The design, layout, and graphics/ illustrations in my calendar are effective and original.	1	2	3	4	5

Comments by Student: _____

_____

_____

_____

Comments by Teacher: _____

_____

_____

_____

Reports Students Love to Write   ©1999 by Incentive Publications, Inc., Nashville, TN.

The Comic Strip Report

The Comic Strip Report may be constructed from a piece of 12" x 18" manila drawing paper. The paper may be folded or divided into eight equal sections or spaces. A research topic is determined and information is gathered and recorded. In its final form, the information is presented through a cartoon character who reports the facts in a comic strip format.

Fold a piece of 12" x 18" manila drawing paper in half from the bottom up, then open and fold it in half the other way. Fold it once more to make a total of eight equal sections. Trace the creases and divide the sections with a black crayon or marker.

Select an academic subject to research, and take notes from your readings. Decide on the most important facts, concepts, and ideas to be written about in the comic strip report. Create a cartoon character that is in some way related to the topic.

Write the title and a brief description of what the report is all about in the first section of the comic strip. In the remaining seven sections, create the comic, using graphics, balloons, and other comic strip elements to present facts from your research.

Planning Guide for the Comic Strip Report

Name: _____

Topic: _____

1	2
3	4
5	6
7	8

©1999 by Incentive Publications, Inc., Nashville, TN.

Assessment Rubric

	Best	Next Best	Keep Working
1. Quality of Report Format Comic report is in 8 sections (the first section with title and description of report). Relevant cartoon character reports information on topic with graphics, balloons, etc.	♥♥♥	♥♥	♥
2. Quality of Information Relevant and key information is clearly conveyed in a logical sequence.	♥♥♥	♥♥	♥
3. Grammar Comic strip is without grammar or spelling errors.	♥♥♥	♥♥	♥
4. Interest The comic strip report is interesting and engaging.	♥♥♥	♥♥	♥
5. Graphics/Creativity Comic includes colorful and creative graphics and drawings.	♥♥♥	♥♥	♥

Comments by Student: _____

_____

_____

_____

Comments by Teacher: _____

_____

_____

_____

Reports Students Love to Write

The Cube Report Arranged According to Bloom's Taxonomy

Bloom's Taxonomy is a structure for the teaching and learning of thinking skills. The six levels (sequentially arranged from lower- to higher-order thinking skills) are Knowledge, Comprehension, Application, Analysis, Synthesis, and Evaluation. Since cubes have six sides and information can be recorded on all six sides, the cube offers a unique format for using Bloom's Taxonomy to organize and present an interesting and informative report. Cubes can be constructed from existing boxes in various sizes, or from boxes made from posterboard or oak tag. If printed cardboard boxes are used, it is suggested they be covered with paper so that the recorded information will be easy to read and study.

There are four steps in developing a cube report:

1. Select a topic.
2. Do research on the topic, and summarize and organize it according to Bloom's Taxonomy.
3. Construct the cube.
4. Print or type the information on poster or typing paper and paste on the six sides of the cube.

A cube may be made by covering a box with butcher or wrapping paper, or building a new cube using the pattern provided on the next page. If the second option is selected, enlarge the cube pattern so that the report will be more readable.

Note: The cube report lends itself especially well to book reports.

Pattern to Use for the Cube Report

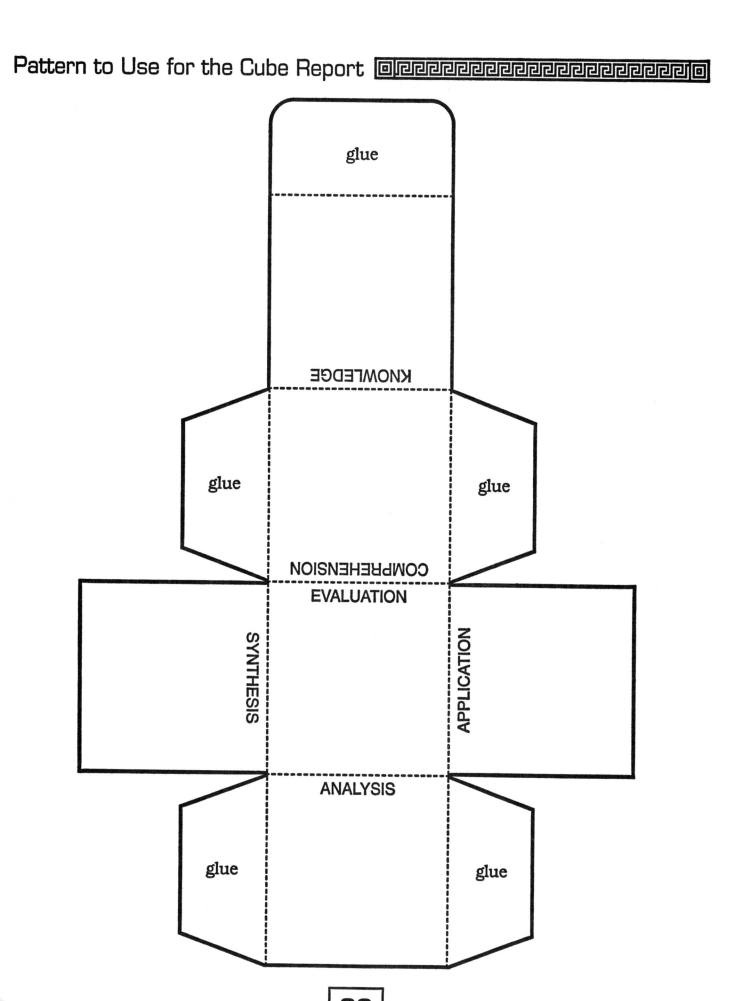

Reports Students Love to Write

Cube Report

Rating Scale

☆   ☆☆   ☆☆☆   ☆☆☆☆

---

1. Quality of Report Format
Cube has relevant topic information neatly written or typed on all six sides.

Rating: _____

---

2. Quality of Information
Important information is clearly conveyed.

Rating: _____

---

3. Grammar
The grammar and spelling of the cube report is good.

Rating: _____

---

4. Interest
The cube is an attractive and interesting presentation of the topic.

Rating: _____

---

5. Graphics/Creativity
The cube is well constructed and neatly put together.

Rating: _____

Comments by Student: _____

_____

_____

_____

Comments by Teacher: _____

_____

_____

_____

Reports Students Love to Write   ©1999 by Incentive Publications, Inc., Nashville, TN.

The Diary or Journal Report

Journals and diaries have always been a great way to record information about everything from personal tragedies to memoirs of explorations and discoveries. "Dear Diary" conversations can report on one's innermost ideas or reflections on a given topic or concept. Diaries tend to record events, emotions, and reactions that are affective or personal in nature. Journals tend to be used to record factual observations, experiences, and findings that are more cognitive or academic in nature. Both diary and journal entries bear dates, but diary entries are often recorded daily while journal entries may be more sporadic.

Once a topic has been selected, the student will decide whether to use the diary or the journal format to record research findings. If a diary format is desired, the student will write daily entries about the topic, being sure to record important events, activities, introspective feelings, and reactions to the information collected. If a journal format is selected, the student will write periodic entries about the topic, being sure to record observations and experiences as well as to write summaries, conclusions, and descriptions.

Planning Guide for the **Diary or Journal Report**

Name: _____

Topic: _____ Date: _____

Dear Diary/Journal,

_____

_____

_____

_____

_____

_____

_____

_____

_____

_____

_____

_____

_____

_____

_____

_____

_____

_____

_____

_____

_____

_____

_____

_____

_____

_____

Closing or Signature: _____

Assessment Rubric

Rating Scale

0 = Not evident   **1** = Slightly evident   **2** = Evident   **3** = Very evident!

1. Quality of Report Format

My diary or journal report records dated entries about my topic (whether important events, activities, feelings, reactions to information, observations, experiences, summaries, conclusions, or descriptions).

Rating: _____

2. Quality of Information

My diary or journal is well researched and conveys important information on my topic.

Rating: _____

3. Grammar

There are no errors in the grammar and spelling of my report.

Rating: _____

4. Interest

My report is interesting to read and holds the reader's attention.

Rating: _____

5. Graphics/Creativity

The information in my report is creatively organized and presented.

Rating: _____

Comments by Student: _____

_____

_____

_____

Comments by Teacher: _____

_____

_____

_____

Reports Students Love to Write

Flash and Fact Card Reports

A Flash Card Report and a Fact Card Report are similar in that each has detailed information about a concept on one side and something else—either a graphic or a title—on the other side. Flash Card Reports are designed around a common research topic or theme. Important facts, definitions, or concepts are described in detail on one side of the card in paragraph form; the titles of the ideas are printed in large letters on the opposite side of the card. These Flash Cards may be used as an aid for learning new information or for reviewing old information. Fact Card Reports are also designed around a special research topic. Like the Flash Cards, a Fact Card has detailed information written on one side of the card, but the title is written just above the paragraph. A common symbol, design, or graphic is placed on the back of the Fact Cards so that all the cards look alike. These Fact Cards can serve double duty as game cards for learning games such as Concentration. If some of the Fact Cards are duplicated, they can be used to play games such as Fish or Rummy.

Flash and Fact Cards are most easily constructed by using 4" x 6" file cards. Once a topic has been selected and researched, important pieces of information are written in paragraph form on one side of each card. This information should be a combination of relevant subject-oriented ideas, interesting definitions of terms, and explanations of major concepts, all related to the common theme.

When creating a series of Flash Cards, it is important to put the title of the paragraph on one side of the card so that each card is different from every other card.

When creating a series of Fact Cards, decide on a special graphic that relates to the report topic and that can serve as an organizing theme for the Fact Cards.

Planning Guide for **Flash and Fact Card Reports**

Name: _____

Topic: _____

Reports Students Love to Write

Flash and Fact Card Report

Assessment Rubric

Rating Scale

WOW!

OK

BOO-HOO!

1. Quality of Report Format
My set of Flash Cards or Fact Cards conveys detailed topic information on my topic on 4" x 6" cards.

Rating: _____

2. Quality of Information
My cards convey well-researched key information on my topic, including facts, definitions, and concepts in paragraph form.

Rating: _____

3. Grammar
My cards display perfect grammar and spelling.

Rating: _____

4. Interest
My cards present information in an attractive and entertaining way.

Rating: _____

5. Graphics/Creativity
The construction of my cards is of good quality and the graphics on them are accomplished and relevant.

Rating: _____

Comments by Student: _____

_____

_____

_____

Comments by Teacher: _____

_____

_____

_____

Game Report

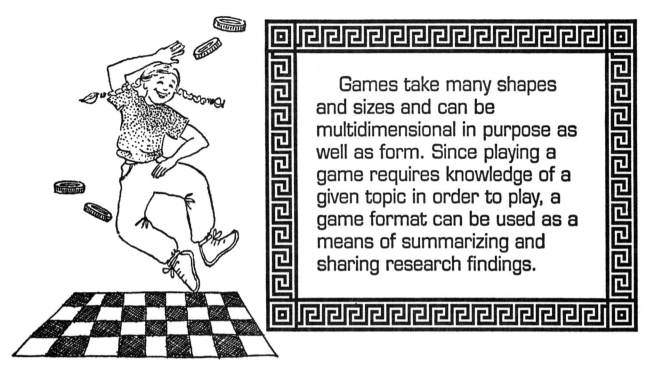

Games take many shapes and sizes and can be multidimensional in purpose as well as form. Since playing a game requires knowledge of a given topic in order to play, a game format can be used as a means of summarizing and sharing research findings.

The student should determine the type of game he or she wants to construct before a topic is selected for research. There are board games, card games, outdoor games, television games, and action games. Board games and card games are often the best choices for a written report because they provide the designer and the players with a format that allows key terms, concepts, and data to be recorded.

Before getting started, the student should review several popular commercial board and card games to stimulate ideas. Then the student can select a topic and conduct research on the topic. He or she can create several game elements to convey or apply the information learned. It is important that there be enough content in the game so that knowledge will be a key to winning and learning will take place as the game is played. Some steps for constructing good-quality board games are outlined below.

A. Plan the Game.

1. Determine the topic for your Game Report. A social studies topic might take a look at people in history; a language arts topic might be an investigation of reference books; a math topic can present a function that requires practice; a science topic may be a presentation of a particular branch of science.

2. Think of a creative title for your game, such as "American Heroes," "Thesaurus Therapy," "Decimal Dodgery," "Chemistry Creations"...

3. Determine the number of players.

4. Define the object or purpose of the game. It should be a dual purpose. The object of the game itself may be to advance a playing piece a certain number of squares by answering questions correctly. The learning purpose of the same game may be to present information on a given topic or to provide a means of practicing skills.

5. Decide whether you will need dice or a spinner.

6. Think about the playing pieces for the players and what they can be made of: bottle caps, pebbles, wooden cubes, coins, beans, etc.

7. Will there be question cards?

8. Will there be chance or good luck/bad luck cards?

9. Create an answer key or booklet.

10. Think of the rules that would be required for playing the game you envision.

11. Create an idea for a playing board (in an interesting shape if possible). Draw a "rough draft" of the playing board.

12. Think of ideas for packaging the game contents (box, reclosable plastic bag, large envelope, etc.).Sketch or write a description of the game container.

B. Creating the Game

1. Using reference books, make up 20 to 40 questions and/or activity cards. To make the game interesting, add some theme-based chance cards such as "Lost the election: move back two spaces" or "Failed the math test: lose a turn."

2. Copy the rough draft of your game board onto posterboard. Add illustrations, borders, and symbols to make the board attractive and fun.

3. Make or find the playing pieces for the players.

4. Create the game package.

5. Write the rules and directions to be included in the game package. Check to make sure that the following questions are answered:

   a. What is the object of this game?

   b. Who goes first? second? third? etc.

   c. How do players move around the board?

   d. What do players do when they land on a place?

   e. Who checks the answers in the answer booklet or key?

   f. What happens if players answer a question correctly? Incorrectly?

   g. When is the game over?

Planning Guide for the **Game Report**

Name: _____

Topic: _____

1. Topic to be used: _____
_____

2. Creative title: _____
_____

3. Number of players: _____

4. Object or purpose of the game: _____
_____
_____
_____

5. Playing pieces for the game: _____
_____

6. Sample questions: _____
_____
_____
_____
_____

7. Types of chance or good luck/bad luck cards: _____
_____

8. Rules and directions for play: _____
_____
_____
_____
_____

9. Shape/type of board/cards: _____

10. Packaging for game contents: _____
_____

Reports Students Love to Write

▦▦▦▦▦▦▦▦ Assessment Rubric ▦▦▦▦▦▦▦▦

Rating Scale	**+**	**O**	**–**
	WOW!	**OK**	**BOO-HOO!**

1. Quality of Report Format
My report is a game that allows those who play it to learn about my topic.

Rating: _____

2. Quality of Information
My game conveys well-researched, key information on my topic.

Rating: _____

3. Grammar
Any text on my game shows perfect grammar and spelling.

Rating: _____

4. Interest
My game presents the information in an attractive and entertaining way.

Rating: _____

5. Graphics/Creativity
My game uses the elements of my chosen game format creatively and effectively.

Rating: _____

Comments by Student: _____

_____

_____

_____

Comments by Teacher: _____

_____

_____

_____

The Graphic Organizer Report

Graphic organizers are learning aids whose effectiveness depends on the visual organization of information. They have many uses and are especially helpful after knowledge is acquired and needs to be presented in a meaningful, organized way.

A Graphic Organizer Report is centered around a theme or topic. Once the topic has been researched and the information collected, a graphic organizer or set of organizers can be used to record and present the information. The same information can be categorized or structured in several different ways depending on the focus of the report.

When more than one graphic organizer is combined into a single report, the combined organizers can show different dimensions of the research topic. This is an especially effective report format for use with cooperative learning groups or for advanced students' independent study projects.

There are many different types of graphic organizers, with different names. Outlines of the Compare and Contrast diagram, the Organizing Tree, the 5 Ws and How Model, and the Web can be seen on the next two pages.

For comprehensive information on graphic organizers, see *Graphic Organizers and Planning Outlines* by Imogene Forte and Sandra Schurr, Nashville: Incentive Publications, 1997.

Examples of the **Graphic Organizer Report**

Name: _____

Topic: _____

Compare and Contrast Diagram

| Concept 1 _____ | Concept 2 _____ |

HOW ALIKE?

_____
_____
_____
_____

HOW DIFFERENT?
With Regard To

_____	◀▶	_____
_____	◀▶	_____
_____	◀▶	_____
_____		_____

The 5 Ws and How Model

Who:

What:

When:

Where:

Why:

How:

Summary Statement:

Reports Students Love to Write   ©1999 by Incentive Publications, Inc., Nashville, TN.

Examples of the **Graphic Organizer Report**

Organizing Tree

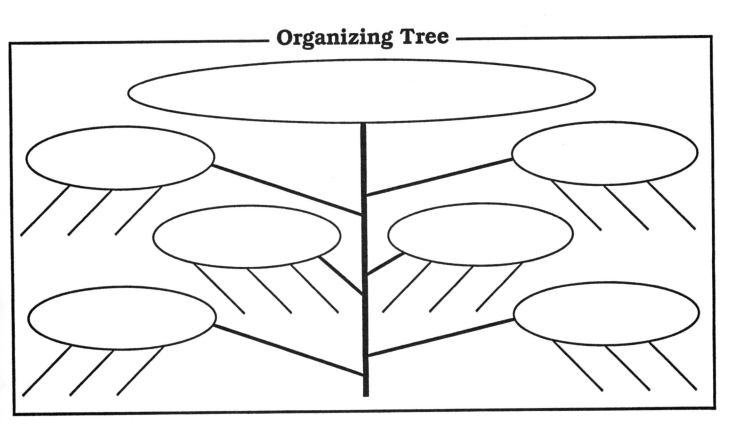

The Web

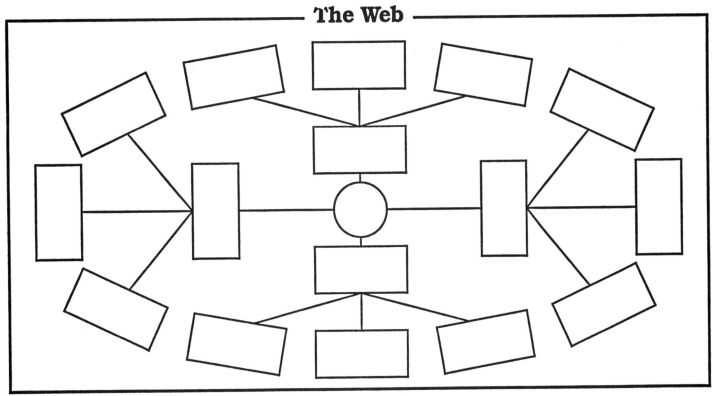

Reports Students Love to Write

The Graphic Organizer Report

Assessment Rubric

1. Quality of Report Format
Each graphic organizer is a good choice for use in the report.

WOW!   Needs More Work

OK

2. Quality of Information
The information shows significant research on the topic.

WOW!   Needs More Work

OK

3. Grammar
There are no spelling or grammar errors.

WOW!   Needs More Work

OK

4. Interest
The different subtopics fit together well and highlight the main points of the topic.

WOW!   Needs More Work

OK

5. Graphics/Creativity
Each graphic organizer fits the information that needs to be conveyed.

WOW!   Needs More Work

OK

Comments by Student: _____

_____

_____

_____

Comments by Teacher: _____

_____

_____

_____

The Learning Poster Report

Based on The Eight Multiple Intelligences as identified by Howard Gardner

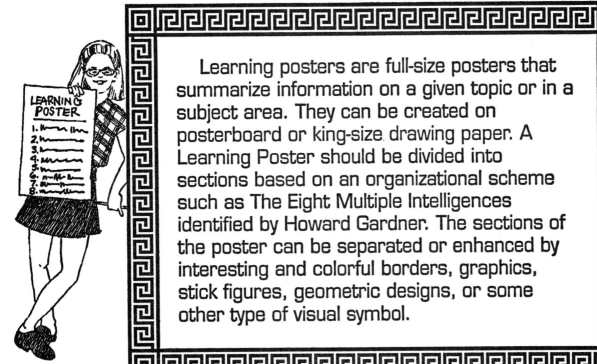

Learning posters are full-size posters that summarize information on a given topic or in a subject area. They can be created on posterboard or king-size drawing paper. A Learning Poster should be divided into sections based on an organizational scheme such as The Eight Multiple Intelligences identified by Howard Gardner. The sections of the poster can be separated or enhanced by interesting and colorful borders, graphics, stick figures, geometric designs, or some other type of visual symbol.

Once a report topic and an organizational scheme have been chosen, the student collects and summarizes information of importance and significance. The information is then organized into sections.

If the Multiple Intelligences are being used as an organizer, each section will present interesting ideas, data, or research findings using one of the intelligences as its focus. For example, a Learning Poster on the topic of the Civil War might have sections written to reflect the following.

Verbal/Linguistic Intelligence: A synthesis of the multiple causes of the Civil War.

Logical/Mathematical Intelligence: A chart comparing the strengths and weaknesses of the Confederate and the Union armies.

Visual/Spatial Intelligence: A timeline of key events related to the Civil War.

Bodily/Kinesthetic Intelligence: A dramatic account of the war conditions for soldiers during a Civil War battle with a suggestion to act out the battle.

Musical Rhythmic Intelligence: A written musical interpretation of a favorite hymn or ballad of the period.

Interpersonal Intelligence: A set of interview questions and possible responses to be made into a dialogue between Thomas Paine and a soldier to be published in the periodical "Common Sense."

Intrapersonal Intelligence: A diary entry by President Lincoln as he is about to deliver the Gettysburg Address.

Natural/Environmental Intelligence: A description of how forests and farmlands were affected by battles during the Civil War.

Multiple Intelligences Planning Guide for a **Learning Poster** 回rerererl回

Name: _____

Topic: _____

Verbal/Linguistic Poster Section:

Verbal/Linguistic intelligence allows one to develop skills related to words and language. A person who is strong in this intelligence may enjoy reading books and may find it easy to write poems or stories, to give talks, and to play word games.

_____

_____

_____

_____

_____

_____

_____

Logical/Mathematical Poster Section:

Logical/Mathematical intelligence, often called "scientific thinking," is the basis of thinking and reasoning skills, numbers skills, and skills in recognizing abstract patterns. A person strong in this intelligence may enjoy science experiments and may find it easy to do mental math operations, to do logic puzzles, and to figure out number and sequence patterns.

_____

_____

_____

_____

_____

_____

_____

Name: _____

Topic: _____

Visual/Spatial Poster Section:

Visual/Spatial intelligence, based on the senses of sight and hearing, enables a student to create mental images and to judge and make use of spatial qualities such as distance and shape. A person strong in this intelligence may prefer reading material that has lots of diagrams or illustrations and may find it easy to draw, paint, build, and follow maps and flow charts.

_____

_____

_____

_____

_____

_____

_____

_____

Bodily/Kinesthetic Poster Section:

Bodily/Kinesthetic intelligence gives rise to skill in various kinds of physical movement. The person high in this intelligence may enjoy sports or other physical activities, working with the hands, dancing, gymnastics, and art work such as sculpture or finger painting that requires touch.

_____

_____

_____

_____

_____

_____

_____

_____

Multiple Intelligences Planning Guide for a **Learning Poster**

Name: _____

Topic: _____

Musical/Rhythmic Poster Section:

Musical/Rhythmic intelligence allows a student to recognize tonal patterns and sounds and to be sensitive to rhythms. The person strong in this intelligence may find it easy to play a musical instrument or sing, remember jingles and lyrics, and compose songs.

_____

_____

_____

_____

_____

_____

_____

Interpersonal Poster Section:

Interpersonal intelligence gives rise to communication skills and skillful handling of person-to-person relationships. A person high in this intelligence probably empathizes well with others and may find it easy to resolve conflicts, lead groups, plan social activities, and teach or counsel others.

_____

_____

_____

_____

_____

_____

_____

Reports Students Love to Write   ©1999 by Incentive Publications, Inc., Nashville, TN.

Multiple Intelligences Planning Guide for a **Learning Poster**

Name: _____

Topic: _____

Intrapersonal Poster Section:

Intrapersonal intelligence allows a student to be aware of inner states of being, to reflect on issues having to do with the self, and to "think about thinking." The person high in this intelligence may keep private diaries or journals, analyze own strengths and weaknesses, set goals, and work independently.

_____

_____

_____

_____

_____

_____

_____

_____

Natural/Environmental Poster Section:

Natural/Environmental intelligence is probably found in the person who is aware of the natural environment, is interested in ways and means of taking care of and responsibly making use of the natural environment, and who is comfortable with and curious about nature and the environment.

_____

_____

_____

_____

_____

_____

_____

©1999 by Incentive Publications, Inc., Nashville, TN.

Reports Students Love to Write

The Learning Poster Report

Assessment Rubric

Quality of Report Format

__ 1 Yes _____ 2 Kind Of _____ 3 No__

1. My Learning Poster is a large poster containing eight sections, one for each Multiple Intelligence approach to my topic/subject.

Quality of Information

__ 1 Yes _____ 2 Kind Of _____ 3 No__

2. The organization of information in my Learning Poster makes logical sense and it covers my topic well.

Grammar

__ 1 Yes _____ 2 Kind Of _____ 3 No__

3. My Learning Poster contains no grammar or spelling errors.

Interest

__ 1 Yes _____ 2 Kind Of _____ 3 No__

4. My Learning Poster uses layout and graphics to make my topic easier to understand and interesting to read.

Graphics/Creativity

__ 1 Yes _____ 2 Kind Of _____ 3 No__

5. My Learning Poster conveys information visually in an original and effective way.

Comments by Student: _____

_____

_____

_____

Comments by Teacher: _____

_____

_____

_____

Letter or Postcard Report

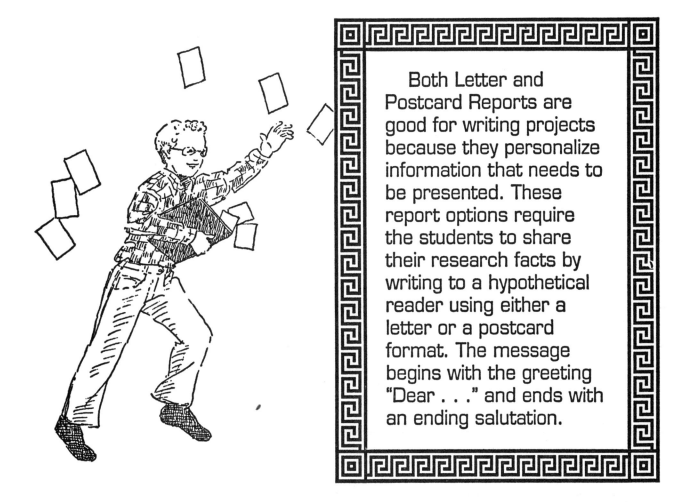

Both Letter and Postcard Reports are good for writing projects because they personalize information that needs to be presented. These report options require the students to share their research facts by writing to a hypothetical reader using either a letter or a postcard format. The message begins with the greeting "Dear . . ." and ends with an ending salutation.

To make a Postcard Report, the student creates a factual message on a card, an imaginary or real address, and, of course, a picture on the opposite side of the card. A Postcard Report usually consists of five to ten postcards on different aspects of the report topic.

Letter Reports require the student to create a series of separate letters written in a logical sequence to the same person on the same topic. It is sometimes desirable to design original stationery for this purpose.

After the student decides on a topic for the report, information is collected and recorded. The postcards or letters should give comprehensive coverage of the important facts of the topic. The letter or postcard messages should be personal, but also informative so that many ideas pertaining to the topic can be discussed. It is necessary to carefully plan the number and nature of the postcards or letters that will complete a high-quality report. Pictures, graphics, and designs should be planned as well.

Planning Guide for the Business Letter Report

Name: _____

Topic: _____

_____

_____

_____

_____

_____

_____

_____

_____

_____

Dear _____:

_____

_____

_____

_____

_____

_____

_____

_____

_____

Sincerely,

_____

Planning Guide for the Business Letter Report Envelope

Name: _____

Topic: _____

Cut on solid lines.
Fold on dotted lines.

Reports Students Love to Write

Name: _____

Topic: _____

Postcard

Stamp

To:

▨▨▨▨▨▨▨▨▨▨▨ Assessment Rubric ▨▨▨▨▨▨▨▨▨▨▨

Rating Scale: 3 = Excellent   2 = Good   1= Fair   0 = No evidence

Elements to Be Evaluated	Letter	Postcard
1. Quality of Report Format My report includes a series of letters or postcards to the same person conveying information on my topic.		
2. Quality of Information The topic information is factual and is conveyed in as many letters/postcards as necessary.		
3. Grammar There are no spelling or grammar errors in my report.		
4. Interest The main points of my topic are explained personally yet informatively, and my letters or postcards follow a logical sequence.		
5. Graphics/Creativity The graphics and designs on my letter stationery or the pictures and scenes on my postcards help communicate the topic information.		

Comments by Student: _____

_____

_____

Comments by Teacher: _____

_____

_____

Reports Students Love to Write

Magazine Biography Report or Photographic Essay Report

Magazine Biography and Photographic Essay Reports are alike in some ways. Each requires research and/or observation to gather information on a subject, and each use pictures as springboards for the presentation of information. The two reports are different in that the Magazine Biography is written about the life of a person while the Photographic Essay is written about a special place or event.

To begin, the student records ten to twenty important facts about the subject and then finds magazine illustrations, creates original graphics, or takes photographs to accompany the facts. There may be a short quiz at the end of the report to assess what the reader has gained from the information.

Once the student has selected an important person or an interesting event or place to research, the facts are gathered and recorded. One key idea or fact is written on each page and is accompanied by an illustration that reflects and enhances the fact. These illustrations may be serious or humorous. The pages are put together in a booklet with a title page. The report should contain a short objective paper-and-pencil test to challenge the reader's ability to remember the information in the report.

Planning Guide for the **Magazine Biography Report** or **Photographic Essay Report**

Name: _____

Topic: _____

Fact One: _____

_____

Fact Two: _____

_____

Fact Three: _____

_____

Fact Four: _____

_____

Fact Five: _____

_____

Fact Six: _____

_____

Fact Seven: _____

_____

Fact Eight: _____

_____

Fact Nine: _____

_____

Fact Ten: _____

_____

Reports Students Love to Write

Magazine Biography Report or Photographic Essay Report

Assessment Rubric

Rating Scale
0 = Not Observed
1 = Tell Me What I'm Doing Wrong!
2 = Tell Me What I Need to Improve!
3 = I'm Doing Terrific!

---

1. Quality of Report Format
My report booklet contains 10 to 20 important facts (one key idea/fact per page) illustrated with magazine illustrations or photographs, along with a title page and a short test.

Rating: _____

---

2. Quality of Information
My report is well researched and conveys important information on my topic.

Rating: _____

---

3. Grammar
There are no errors in grammar and spelling in my report.

Rating: _____

---

4. Interest
My report is interesting to read and the pictures hold the reader's attention.

Rating: _____

---

5. Graphics/Creativity
The magazine illustrations/photographs are appropriate (whether humorously or seriously) for illustrating the information I have learned about my topic.

Rating: _____

Comments by Student: _____

_____

_____

_____

Comments by Teacher: _____

_____

_____

_____

The Matrix Report

A matrix is a tool that allows the student to cross-reference many related ideas at one time.

To create a Matrix Report, the student selects a topic to research and classifies each piece of new information into one of several categories. The matrix consists of an arrangement of multiple cells or boxes; major categories are listed horizontally across the top of the matrix, and a set of related topics is listed vertically down one side of the matrix. The information that is relevant to both sets of descriptors or categories is placed in the appropriate cell.

Once a topic has been selected for research, relevant facts can be recorded on 3" x 5" file cards according to a predetermined set of categories. For example, if the topic of the report is "Famous Women in History", categories may include Name, Birthplace/Date, Character Traits, Obstacles Overcome, Special Accomplishments, and Key Influences. Before creating the matrix on a piece of paper, a king-size matrix can be constructed with the file cards arranged in rows of five across and five down. The information cards for each of the women are arranged in rows to reflect the categories.

Planning Guide for the **Matrix Report**

Name: _____

Topic: _____

Assessment Rubric

Rating Scale:

Well Done ← Medium → Needs More

1. Quality of Report Format The Matrix Report includes appropriate categories and information in rows and columns.	
2. Quality of Information The information in my report demonstrates significant research into the topic.	
3. Grammar There are no spelling or grammar errors in my report.	
4. Interest The different elements and comparative features in my matrix highlight the main points of my topic and explain the topic well.	
5. Graphics/Creativity The layout and selection of information is creative and original.	

Comments by Student: _____

_____

_____

_____

Comments by Teacher: _____

_____

_____

_____

The Mural Report

A mural report is often completed by a small group of six to eight students who create the mural as a collaborative report. It may also be the work of one student who will use it as an individual report, or of two or three students who choose it as a product for authentic assessment of an independent study project. If it is used for a group report, the group decides on a topic, assigns different research tasks to each group member, and cooperatively outlines both the information and the illustrations to be included in the mural.

The mural should be created on a large piece of rolled paper often found in the art room of a school or in an artist's supplies shop. The mural should be divided into sections, and it should be colorful and informative.

Once the group has decided on a research topic, students may volunteer to gather information on different elements of the topic. The students should take notes while researching, and informally share their information with the others in the group. The group then divides a piece of king-size mural paper into multiple sections so that there is one space for each group member. Each student writes and illustrates the ideas for his or her assigned section, using the notes written during the research phase. Each section of the mural should be placed in a logical sequence so that the ideas are clear and accurate.

Name: _____

Topic: _____

Overall Theme of Mural:

Assigned Topic for Mural: _____

_____

Ideas for My Mural Section: _____

_____

_____

_____

_____

_____

Sketch of Graphic for My Section:

Assessment Rubric

Quality of Report Format

First base	Second base	Third Base	Home Run!

1. Our mural report is made of one mural divided into sections, one section for each group member. Each section uses text and graphics to illustrate a portion of the topic.

Quality of Information

First base	Second base	Third Base	Home Run!

2. The information in our mural is organized in a logical sequence and is presented well to convey key information on our topic.

Grammar

First base	Second base	Third Base	Home Run!

3. Our mural report contains no grammar or spelling errors.

Interest

First base	Second base	Third Base	Home Run!

4. Our report uses the mural format to make our topic easier to understand and more interesting to learn.

Graphics/Creativity

First base	Second base	Third Base	Home Run!

5. Our mural is attractive and creative.

Comments by Student: _____

_____

_____

_____

Comments by Teacher: _____

_____

_____

_____

The Newspaper Report

Read all about it!

The newspaper format is an excellent structure for reporting information on any topic of interest or unit of study. Newspaper Reports require the student to select a theme that can be presented using the major parts of a typical newspaper. Newspaper Reports can include information that reflects a news story, a feature story, an editorial, a classified ad, a comic strip, a review, and even a business, entertainment, or sports-related section.

To be most effective, a Newspaper Report should be written on a long piece of shelf paper so that all sections can be visible at one glance. The piece of shelf paper should have a wide banner headline at the top and should be divided into two long columns by a line drawn down the middle. Each article or section of the newspaper should have its own space separated from the rest by a thin border or frame.

Once a topic has been determined, the student should gather the necessary information and write about it using the newspaper formats of feature stories, news stories, editorials, letters to the editor, ads, comic strips, reviews, and business or sports commentaries.

Color and graphics may be used to enhance the newspaper's appearance. The masthead of the newspaper should reflect the theme of the report.

Planning Guide for the **Newspaper Report**

Name: _____

Topic: _____

Language Arts/English Ideas:

_____

_____

_____

_____

_____

_____

_____

_____

Science Ideas:

_____

_____

_____

_____

_____

_____

_____

_____

_____

Planning Guide for the **Newspaper Report**

Name: _____

Topic: _____

Math Ideas:

_____

_____

_____

_____

_____

_____

_____

_____

_____

Social Studies Ideas:

_____

_____

_____

_____

_____

_____

_____

_____

_____

Reports Students Love to Write

Assessment Rubric

Rating Scale:

Accomplished ⟵ So-So ⟶ Needs Work

1. Quality of Report Format My Newspaper Report includes a banner headline, columns, and different newspaper sections, all on shelf paper.	
2. Quality of Information The information in my report demonstrates significant research into my topic.	
3. Grammar There are no spelling or grammar errors in my Newspaper Report.	
4. Interest The different sections of my Newspaper Report highlight the main points of my topic and explain them well.	
5. Graphics/Creativity The newspaper layout and illustrations help convey information on my topic.	

Comments by Student: _____

_____

_____

_____

Comments by Teacher: _____

_____

_____

_____

The Notebook Field Report

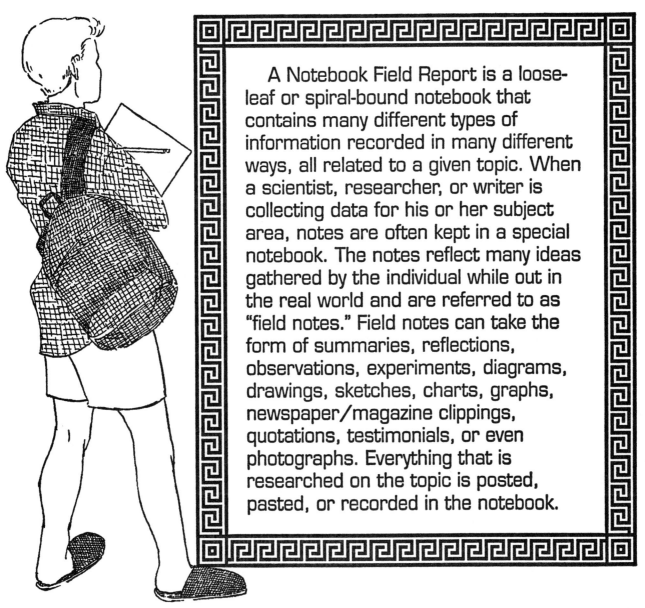

A Notebook Field Report is a loose-leaf or spiral-bound notebook that contains many different types of information recorded in many different ways, all related to a given topic. When a scientist, researcher, or writer is collecting data for his or her subject area, notes are often kept in a special notebook. The notes reflect many ideas gathered by the individual while out in the real world and are referred to as "field notes." Field notes can take the form of summaries, reflections, observations, experiments, diagrams, drawings, sketches, charts, graphs, newspaper/magazine clippings, quotations, testimonials, or even photographs. Everything that is researched on the topic is posted, pasted, or recorded in the notebook.

After a topic has been selected, the student makes or purchases a notebook to be used for collecting all types of information on the topic. This information should take many forms and should be collected from many different sources, including reference books, interviews, encyclopedias, periodicals, the Internet, and observations or interviews in the field.

The material is kept in the notebook according to an organizational structure. For example, it can be organized by subtopic, in chronological order, by importance, or by type of resource. Often the entries are informal and random in thought. It is important that the notebook pages be varied to include everything from penciled notes or clippings to sketches, drawings, or charts. It is also important that all notebook entries be dated and information sources identified.

Planning Guide for the **Notebook Field Report**

Name: _____

Topic: _____

Topic for Notebook: _____

Date Notebook Entries Began: _____

Date Completed Notebook Entries: _____

Directions: Put a checkmark in front of each type of entry resource that is used in the writing of the notebook.

_____ 1.   Information from printed matter such as reference books

_____ 2.   Information from the Internet

_____ 3.   Information from charts/graphs

_____ 4.   Information from diagrams

_____ 5.   Information from sketches or drawings

_____ 6.   Information from interviews

_____ 7.   Information from field observations/visitations

_____ 8.   Information from testimonials

_____ 9.   Information from newspapers/magazines/periodicals

_____ 10.   Information from pictures/photographs/illustrations

_____ 11.   Information from video/movie clips

_____ 12.   Information from other sources (please describe below):

_____

_____

_____

_____

_____

_____

_____

_____

Assessment Rubric

1. Quality of Report Format My report is a notebook recording information on my topic with everything dated and sourced.	Hot!	Warm	Lukewarm	Tepid	Cold
	1	2	3	4	5

2. Quality of Information My field notes show significant research into my topic.	Hot!	Warm	Lukewarm	Tepid	Cold
	1	2	3	4	5

3. Grammar There are no spelling or grammar errors in my notebook.	Hot!	Warm	Lukewarm	Tepid	Cold
	1	2	3	4	5

4. Interest The items in my notebook are diverse and appropriate for presenting key information on my topic.	Hot!	Warm	Lukewarm	Tepid	Cold
	1	2	3	4	5

5. Graphics/Creativity The design, layout, and graphics/illustrations in my notebook are creative and effective.	Hot!	Warm	Lukewarm	Tepid	Cold
	1	2	3	4	5

Comments by Student: _____

_____

_____

_____

Comments by Teacher: _____

_____

_____

_____

Reports Students Love to Write

The Number Report

A Number Report uses numbers instead of the alphabet to organize information. It usually begins with the highest number and ends with the number one; it typically starts with the number ten, although higher or lower numbers may be used depending on the topic.

Once a subject is chosen, the student researches the topic and records a number of facts that reflect directly the numbers used as the report's organizing structure. For example, if the subject of the report is "Pollution" and the numbers one through eight are to be used as the organizing schemata, the planning outline and the facts might line up something like this:

Eight Major Types of Pollution
Seven Key Causes of Pollution
Six Important Dates in the Control of Pollution
Five Reasons to Be Concerned About Pollution
Four Ways You Can Fight Pollution in the Community
Three Little-Known Facts about Recycling
Two Statistics to Remember about Pollution
One Pollution-Related Quotation That Makes Sense

Once a topic has been determined, the numbering schemata to be used to report on the topic must be chosen. The research is conducted and the information is recorded on notecards. Notecards are organized according to the pre-established numbers—if the topic is "Eight Major Types of Pollution," there will be eight different cards, each describing one of the major pollution types.

Notecards should be rewritten so that each card has a good-quality paragraph summarizing the information. Cards are arranged as a "fact file" set of cards. They can be packaged in a file box or fastened together with a rubber band or set of rings. A divider card should be prepared for each number category to organize the ideas for the reader.

Planning Guide for the **Number Report**

Name: _____

Topic: _____

10. _____
_____

9. _____
_____

8. _____
_____

7. _____
_____

6. _____
_____

5. _____
_____

4. _____
_____

3. _____
_____

2. _____
_____

1. _____
_____

Reports Students Love to Write

Assessment Rubric

Quality of Report Format

Very True	True	Somewhat True	Not True

1. My Number Report includes at least ten ample paragraphs summarizing information I learned through researching my topic; it also contains a fact file of notecards.

Quality of Information

Very True	True	Somewhat True	Not True

2. The numerical breakdown of information in my Number Report makes logical sense and is organized well to cover my topic.

Grammar

Very True	True	Somewhat True	Not True

3. My Number Report contains no grammar or spelling errors.

Interest

Very True	True	Somewhat True	Not True

4. My report uses the number format to make my topic easier to understand and interesting to read.

Graphics/Creativity

Very True	True	Somewhat True	Not True

5. My Number Report uses the number format creatively.

Comments by Student: _____

_____

_____

_____

Comments by Teacher: _____

_____

_____

_____

The Placemat Report

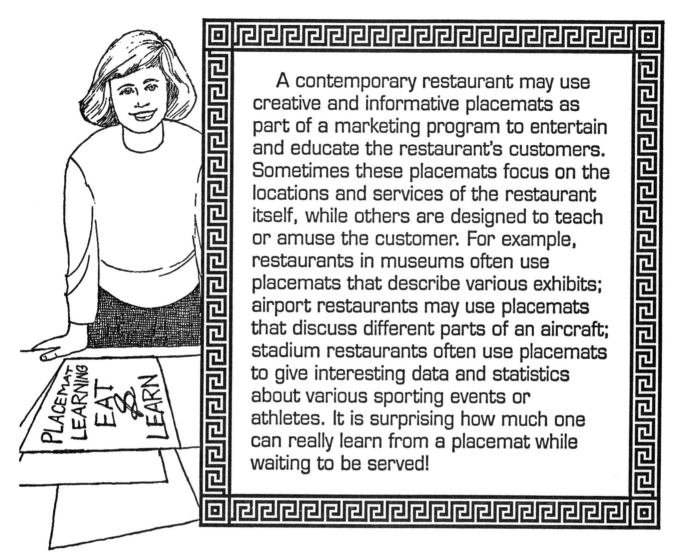

A contemporary restaurant may use creative and informative placemats as part of a marketing program to entertain and educate the restaurant's customers. Sometimes these placemats focus on the locations and services of the restaurant itself, while others are designed to teach or amuse the customer. For example, restaurants in museums often use placemats that describe various exhibits; airport restaurants may use placemats that discuss different parts of an aircraft; stadium restaurants often use placemats to give interesting data and statistics about various sporting events or athletes. It is surprising how much one can really learn from a placemat while waiting to be served!

Instructional placemats should be created to present a specific content and skills base. Each placemat should contain important information to be learned or reviewed as well as a layout that is colorful, interesting, and appropriate for age and ability.

Placemats should be large enough to accommodate a place setting of dishes and silverware and allow for wide borders and extended spaces for graphics or copy. They may be constructed from posterboard, cardstock, drawing paper, or colored construction paper, or even from large pizza boards or box tops. Colored markers, pencils, pens, or crayons may be used for the copy, and clear contact paper may be used as a protective laminate.

Once the topic for the placemat has been determined and researched, the information should be written, drawn, or presented in a condensed form for easy reference. Layout of the information, related graphics, and a summary of content and concepts will complete the placemat.

The Placemat Report

Name: _____

Topic: _____

Assessment Rubric

Rating Scale

| 4 = Excellent | 3 = Good | 2 = Fair | 1 = Poor |

---

1. Quality of Report Format
The placemat conveys information on my topic very well.

Rating: _____

---

2. Quality of Information
My topic was well researched and the placemat conveys a large amount of information.

Rating: _____

---

3. Grammar
The grammar and spelling of my placemat is good.

Rating: _____

---

4. Interest
The placemat is attractive and entertaining.

Rating: _____

---

5. Graphics/Creativity
The graphics, images, design, and layout of my placemat are of high quality.

Rating: _____

Comments by Student: _____

_____

_____

_____

Comments by Teacher: _____

_____

_____

_____

Reports Students Love to Write

Question-and-Answer Flip-and-Tell Report

The Question-and-Answer Flip-and-Tell Report is written as a series of questions and answers on a given topic. One chooses a subject to research, generates a series of questions, and then looks for the answers in a variety of reference sources. The report is structured so that the pages are staggered. A question is written along the bottom of each page. The response to the question is written on the rest of the page, which is invisible when the book is closed. Needless to say, the longest or hardest questions should be written on the longer pages.

After a topic for the report has been chosen, a set of questions about the topic is developed. Research is conducted to find answers to the questions. To make the staggered flip report booklet, the student determines the number of pages based on the number of questions.

The student uses a ruler to mark off a strip at the bottom of each page so that it is one inch shorter than the one underneath it. For example, the back page should be a full-size piece of paper and equal in size to the back cover. The page directly on top of the back page should be cut one inch shorter in length. The process is repeated for each page, with the first page being the smallest.

When all pages have been cut, they should be stapled together at the top, from smallest to largest, to produce a staggered effect.

The student should write a question along the bottom edge of each page, making sure that the easiest questions with the shortest answers are on the shorter pages and the hardest questions with the longest answers are on the longer pages. An answer to each question is written on the upper part of the same page for each question.

The title of the report should be on the front cover along with the author's name.

Question-and-Answer **Flip-and-Tell Report** ▣▣▣▣▣▣▣▣▣▣▣◨

Name: _____

Topic: _____

Questions to research:

_____

_____

_____

_____

_____

_____

_____

_____

_____

_____

_____

_____

_____

To Make a Flip-and-Tell Report:

- Determine the number of pages based on the number of questions
- Back page is a full-size sheet of paper
- Each page added is one inch shorter than the one before
- The question goes at the bottom of the page and the answer goes at the top of the same page
- The easiest questions on the shorter sheets
- The most difficult questions with longer answers on the longer sheets
- Staple the pages, including back and front covers, to produce a staggered effect with shortest on top and longest on the bottom

83

Assessment Rubric

1. Quality of Report Format
My report is a Question-and-Answer Flip-and-Tell booklet with questions and answers on staggered pages.

2. Quality of Information
The organization of information in my booklet makes logical sense.

3. Grammar
My booklet contains no grammar or spelling errors.

4. Interest
My booklet's layout and graphics make my topic easier to understand and interesting to read about.

5. Graphics/Creativity
My booklet conveys information in an original and effective way.

Comments by Student: _____

_____

_____

_____

Comments by Teacher: _____

_____

_____

_____

Storyboard Chalk Talk Report

A storyboard consists of several frames that are numbered and arranged in sequence to present information on a given subject. Underneath each frame of the storyboard are lines for explaining the illustration that is drawn in each frame. Storyboards are great for planning a "chalk talk." Chalk talks are informative mini-speeches that require the presenter to draw a picture, diagram, or detail on the chalkboard as he or she discusses key ideas of the subject. The storyboard provides a visual plan that coordinates each major concept with a corresponding graphic. If a storyboard is used for planning, by the time the presenter reaches the end of the speech the audience will have seen a coherent presentation given in a logical sequence.

The storyboard set of frames can be used to plan a mini-speech on a special topic or theme. Each major concept of the researched subject is written in one frame of the storyboard along with some detail or component of the intended illustration. It is important to structure the report so that a meaningful graphic accompanies each major idea to be presented. The ultimate goal is to finish both the oral delivery of content and the last detail of the visual scenario at the same time.

Storyboard/Chalk Talk Report

Name: _____

Topic: _____

Assessment Rubric

Quality of Report Format

YES!!	That'll Work	NOT!!

1. My chalk talk is a short speech based on a storyboard with numbered frames, illustrations, and explanations of my topic.

Quality of Information

YES!!	That'll Work	NOT!!

2. The data in my chalk talk is researched well and presented in a logical sequence.

Grammar

YES!!	That'll Work	NOT!!

3. My storyboard and chalk talk contain no grammar or spelling errors.

Interest

YES!!	That'll Work	NOT!!

4. My chalk talk and storyboard make my topic easier to understand and interesting to learn about.

Graphics/Creativity

YES!!	That'll Work	NOT!!

5. My chalk talk and storyboard use visuals and graphics creatively and effectively.

Comments by Student: _____

_____

_____

_____

Comments by Teacher: _____

_____

_____

_____

The Tape-Recorded Report

In preparation for the Tape-recorded Report the student selects the topic and conducts the research necessary for the report. Notes are recorded on file cards to be used to sequentially organize the ideas for easy delivery of definitions, events, or concepts. These notes are recorded by the reporter on an audiotape. The notecards may then become a script for the listener.

The student should select a topic that lends itself to being recorded for an audience. The student researches the topic, being sure to put each major idea on a separate file card. The ideas are then arranged in a logical sequence and read into a tape recorder. After each major idea is presented, the reader should pause to allow the listener time for reflection. A question, summary sentence, or startling statement might be used at the end of each major idea for emphasis, challenge, or motivation.

For added interest, one might include a note-taking sheet, a quiz, or a worksheet for the listener to complete while hearing or finishing the "report on tape."

Planning Guide for the **Tape-Recorded Report**

Name: _____

Topic: _____

Major Idea One to Discuss: _____
_____
_____

Major Idea Two to Discuss: _____
_____
_____

Major Idea Three to Discuss: _____
_____
_____

Major Idea Four to Discuss: _____
_____
_____

Major Idea Five to Discuss: _____
_____
_____

Major Idea Six to Discuss: _____
_____
_____

Major Idea Seven to Discuss: _____
_____
_____

Major Idea Eight to Discuss: _____
_____
_____

Major Idea Nine to Discuss: _____
_____
_____

Major Idea Ten to Discuss: _____
_____
_____

Reports Students Love to Write

Assessment Rubric

Quality of Report Format

Off Target	Pretty Close	Near Miss	Bull's Eye

1. My report is an audio recording of notes from my research on my topic, explaining key definitions, events, and concepts.

Quality of Information

Off Target	Pretty Close	Near Miss	Bull's Eye

2. The data in my report is researched well and presented in a logical sequence.

Grammar

Off Target	Pretty Close	Near Miss	Bull's Eye

3. My report contains no grammar errors, and my notecards contain no spelling or grammar errors.

Interest

Off Target	Pretty Close	Near Miss	Bull's Eye

4. My report makes my topic easier to understand and interesting to learn about.

Graphics/Creativity

Off Target	Pretty Close	Near Miss	Bull's Eye

5. My report is given with a clear and engaging voice as well as connections and pauses between notecards.

Comments by Student: _____

_____

_____

_____

Comments by Teacher: _____

_____

_____

_____

Timeline Report

Timelines are excellent tools for writing certain types of reports that deal with important events, how-to tasks, or sequences of future activities. They are vehicles for recording and illustrating important things in chronological order. A timeline uses equal increments of time as benchmark measures. Timelines are best constructed on long strips of shelf paper. They should include key dates, descriptions, and related illustrations for each entry.

To begin this type of report, the student chooses a subject, researches the information, and organizes the data according to important dates over an extended period of time. The Timeline Report should be written on a long piece of shelf paper and should contain three elements for each entry: the date, a paragraph of description for an event or task, and a simple graphic related to the event or task. Timelines should contain at least eight different dates and pieces of related information.

Planning Outline for the **Timeline Report**

Name: _____

Topic: _____

Reports Students Love to Write   ©1999 by Incentive Publications, Inc., Nashville, TN.

▨▨▨▨▨▨▨▨▨▨ Assessment Rubric ▨▨▨▨▨▨▨▨▨▨

Quality of Report Format

On Your Mark	You're Getting There . . .	You've Got It!

1. My timeline includes at least eight benchmarks, with dates, paragraph descriptions of events/tasks, and graphics for each one, organized according to date on a piece of shelf paper.

Quality of Information

On Your Mark	You're Getting There . . .	You've Got It!

2. The data in my timeline is researched well and presented in a logical way.

Grammar

On Your Mark	You're Getting There . . .	You've Got It!

3. My timeline report contains no grammar or spelling errors.

Interest

On Your Mark	You're Getting There . . .	You've Got It!

4. My timeline makes my topic easier to understand and interesting to read.

Graphics/Creativity

On Your Mark	You're Getting There . . .	You've Got It!

5. My timeline report uses the format creatively.

Comments by Student: _____

_____

_____

_____

Comments by Teacher: _____

_____

_____

_____

Reports Students Love to Write

Planning Guide for

Reports that Students Love to Write and Teachers Love to Read

1. **Purpose and Description** (What you hope to accomplish and what the finished report will look like, information it will include, and special features.)

_____

_____

_____

_____

2. **Resources Needed** (Things you will need for the report and sources for securing them.)

_____

_____

_____

3. **Timeline** (Time plan for completing the report, including specific goals and due dates.)

_____

_____

_____

4. **Method for Presentation and Assessment** (How your report will be presented and criteria to be used in evaluating its quality and effectiveness.)

_____

_____

_____

5. **Personal Notes**

_____

_____

_____

Name: _____Date: _____

A Checklist for Reviewing

The Final Draft of A Report A Teacher Will Love to Read

Name: _____

Topic: _____

_____ 1. Have I identified my reader and is my work interesting and/or informative to the reader?

_____ 2. Have I presented my thoughts, ideas, and information in a logical sequential manner?

_____ 3. Have I used words that I know and understand? Will they be understood by my intended reader?

_____ 4. Have I eliminated unnecessary, confusing, or irrelevant words or phrases (or even sentences) from my work?

_____ 5. Have I eliminated overused words or phrases, and have I avoided clichés?

_____ 6. Have I used examples, illustrations, or analogies to explain or clarify main ideas or important concepts?

_____ 7. Have I used some unusual or extraordinary descriptive words or phrases that add interest to my work?

_____ 8. Have I included all necessary information and related details?

_____ 9. Have I included a good balance of different kinds of sentences to maintain the reader's interest throughout my work?

_____ 10. Have I checked my spelling, grammar, and punctuation carefully?

_____ 11. Is my ending interesting enough to leave my reader with a better understanding of my subject, some new ideas, and/or thoughts to ponder?

_____ 12. Is my writing neat, clear, easy to read, and representative of my best work?

_____ 13. Is this report representative of my absolute best work?

Adapted with permission from *Reading and Writing Success Student Planner and Study Guide*, Incentive Publications, Nashville, TN, 1997